ISLAMIC PATTERNS

J. BOURGOIN

Dover Publications, Inc., New York

Publisher's Note

By forbidding the representation of the human figure, the Mohammedan religion helped push Islamic art along a path much different from that of traditional European art. European painting and drawing abounds with perspective renderings of figures and landscapes, whereas Islamic art translates artistic impulse into elaborate geometric patterns and linear designs. Through centuries of practicing this purely abstract art, Muslim artists have perfected it to an incomparable elegance.

The 45 elaborate full-page patterns in this book are all adapted from illustrations published in a late nineteenth-century pictorial album edited by J. Bourgoin, a noted French art historian. They demonstrate the inventiveness of the Muslim artists, who are able to transform such simple geometrical forms as squares, triangles, circles and regular polygons into countless incredibly beautiful patterns.

These intricate designs are great fun to work with because they provide each artist with an opportunity to create uniquely personal artworks. Some artists may choose to emphasize the pattern's great complexity by picking out each distinct geometrical form in a different color, whereas others may wish to point up the underlying unity of the design by emphasizing the basic, regularly repeating motif. The colored examples printed on the covers of this book are meant merely as a suggestion; feel free to use these endlessly fascinating patterns in any way you choose.

EAST SUSSEX

| V | KBC | INV No. | 5 0 0 0 1 |

SHELF MARK	
COPY NO.	
BRN	
DATE	LOC	LOC	LOC	LOC	LOC	LOC

COUNTY LIBRARY

Copyright © 1977 by Dover Publications, Inc.
All rights reserved under Pan American and International Copyright Conventions.
Published in Canada by General Publishing Company, Ltd.,
30 Lesmill Road, Don Mills, Toronto, Ontario.

Islamic Patterns, as published by Dover Publications, Inc., in 1986, is a slightly revised republication, incorporating all 45 plates, of the work originally published by Dover in 1977 under the title *Islamic Patterns: An Infinite Design Coloring Book,* which was a slightly revised republication of 45 plates from *Arabic Geometrical Pattern and Design,* published by Dover in 1973.

DOVER *Pictorial Archive* SERIES

This book belongs to the Dover Pictorial Archive Series. You may use the designs and illustrations for graphics and crafts applications, free and without special permission, provided that you include no more than four in the same publication or project. (For permission for additional use, please write to Dover Publications, Inc., 31 East 2nd Street, Mineola, N.Y. 11501.)

However, republication or reproduction of any illustration by any other graphic service, whether it be in a book or in any other design resource, is strictly prohibited.

International Standard Book Number: 0-486-23537-8

Manufactured in the United States of America
Dover Publications, Inc.
31 East 2nd Street
Mineola, N.Y. 11501

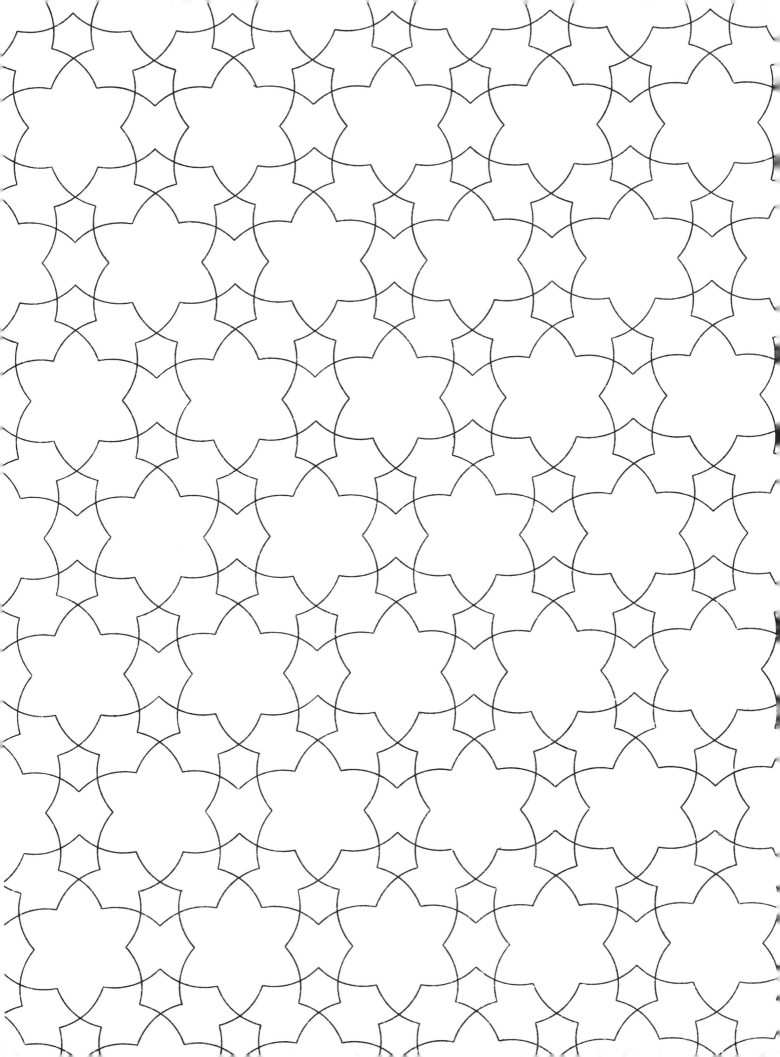